MERICA A. GREEN

Copyright ©2018 Merica A. Green

Editors: Connected By Design, LLC and Arthur L. Green, III

Cover Design: Write The Vision Designs

All rights reserved. No part of this book may be used or reproduced by any means, graphic, electronic, or mechanical, including photocopying, recording, taping or by any information storage retrieval system without the written permission of the publisher except in the case of brief quotations embodied in critical articles and reviews.

Scripture taken from the Holy Bible, NKJV.

Books may be ordered through booksellers or by contacting:

Connected By Design, LLC

connectedbydesign@outlook.com

MERICA A. GREEN

ISBN: 978-0-578-20235-8

Publisher:

Merica G.

Printed in the United States of America

Table of Contents

Dedication

Foreword

Introduction

1. The Essence of Your But

2. The Dis-Qualifier

3. The Distortion of Your But

4. Clear Your Headspace

5. Kiss Your But Goodbye – The Final Battle

6. A Time of Reflection

   From the Author

   Additional Worksheets

Dedication

God, I want to thank You for the confidence to pen what it is that You have placed in my heart so long ago. Thank You for trusting me with this message of encouragement for those that You intend to be readers or hearers of the words contained in the pages that follow. I love You Lord, more than life.

Mommy, you have been my biggest supporter for the last 40 years (my entire life) and I love you for that. Thank you for always being there and for never second guessing my many endeavors in life. I will ever remember the sermon you delivered titled, "Shattering Your Glass Ceiling". This was a powerful and eye-opening message wherein you gave a different perspective of the glass ceiling by highlighting those hindrances that may be so pervasive in an individual's life that they accept them as the norm.

We are able to see beyond where we are to the place that is unattainable because of the hindrances – the glass ceiling – the transparent or translucent, hard, brittle substance between us and that place. I left that sermon understanding that as I shatter my glass ceiling(s), as I press beyond those hindrances, I can expect to be cut and even shed some blood. I can expect to make a mess and even be left with some scars. I can also expect, though, to soar beyond where I am or ever have been and finally, without restraint, begin the path to my destiny.

Mommy, you have always encouraged and challenged my thought process and I thank you. I am blessed beyond measure to have you as my mom and my best friend.

Jackie, Gina, Art, and Erica, you all are the greatest siblings a person could ever hope for. I love you so much and am grateful for the bond we share. I'd run to the moon and back for each of you and know you would do the same for me.

Joseph, Tricia, Brandon, Devon, Lizzie, Chad, and Blake, I find it impossible to believe there are more intelligent, more respectful, more loving children than you. Having you as my nephews and nieces has opened my heart in such a way that can only be expressed through deep emotions (words escape me). I love you all so much and trust that God's best for you will be continually unfolded in your lives and in the lives of your future families.

Foreword

Merica Green boldly stands in the office of an inspirational and motivating coach to those who rely on excuses as their reason not to move forward. She's inspirational in that she has the unique ability to arouse confidence and determination in the heart of the person who struggles with low self-esteem and lack of resilience.

Merica has proven to be motivational through the observation of her own life journey. Regardless of challenges or setbacks, she has always managed to come back and excel further than mediocre expectations. Hence, she is able to motivate across gender and cultural lines, refusing to give permission for you to quit or become stifled in your quest.

Isn't it strange how one can see what they desire in life but allow fear, anxiety, and offense to dismiss their pursuit of acquiring their vision? The principles shared in this book will forcefully eject the reader from this unfavorable location. Every word will chip away at the plan that was intended to keep you shackled and imprisoned. You will discover that the key to your successful future has not been thrown away in the history of time. Rather, the key to unlocking your dreams and making them a reality, lies within you.

Merica magnificently exposes the primary enemy of your destiny, excuses. She doesn't give you permission to use this as a disguise or explanation to remain where you are. Rather, she highlights every reason you have to advance to where you want to be. Her ultimate command for the reader is to, "Get your head out of your *BUT!*" Let's be honest; the title of this book is likely the reason you made the investment. Good news. The return on your investment will be productive.

When the phrase, "Get your head out of your butt" is articulated in a traditional fashion the word "butt" is spelled with two t's, referring to a person's buttocks. It often conveys the message that a person needs to become more aware of their surroundings or stop being so much into themselves that they become conceited. In this book, Merica masterfully helps the reader recognize the excuses that impede their current environment, provides strategies to conquer the excuses, and recommends how one should properly manage the success of overcoming their "but." The content of this book is intended to change the trajectory of the reader's life and help to avoid becoming self-absorbed once the identified *but* has been defeated.

I'm certain that you will feel Merica's passion for people and drive for purpose as you turn the pages of this book. Allow the words to penetrate your soul and move you beyond excuses to aggressively pursuing your dreams.

Lawanne' S. Grant, Ph.D.
Owner of Leadership DevelopME, LLC
www.leadershipdevelopme.com

Introduction

…don't allow your "but" to add unnecessary complexities to this already existing obstacle course called life…

The idiom "get your head out of the clouds" has long been considered a reality check for the daydreamer. It does not suggest that one is literally walking about with their head stuck in a visible mass of condensed vapor floating in the atmosphere. Rather, a person whose head is stuck in the clouds is thought to hang out in the realm of fantasy or anyplace far enough from reality that they can let their minds roam freely without the limits or bonds of reality. Creativity is bred from the imagination of one whose head is in the clouds. Therefore, having your head in the clouds may not always be a bad thing.

However, having your head in your "but" begets no creative prose and stems from an inability to overcome ill begotten rationales – more frequently referred to as EXCUSES. A mind or lifestyle consumed with excuses is a limited, restricted, unfruitful existence. In fact, excuses do nothing more than lull to sleep the chase for and the attainment of your destiny. The pursuit of your purpose and the motivation of your mission become overshadowed by the riddling justification of your "but" and the continuum of "but" leads to the repetition of never manifested dreams and frustrated passion as you remind yourself of why you can never be what it is that God intended for you from your conception in your mother's womb.

In this book, I'd like to walk with you to expose the root cause of your "but" and encourage you to overcome every excuse that ever has, does now, or might attempt in the future to hold you hostage to your "but". Just being human can often be challenging enough…don't allow your "but" to add unnecessary complexities to this already existing obstacle course called life. Come to understand that the "but" in your life could have been superimposed upon you by your family, society, or even by your genetic make-up. No matter how this slippery nay-sayer came to be, it is incumbent upon you to excommunicate excuses and determine today to ***get your head out of your "but"***.

Chapter One

The Essence of Your But

∽

...I was never driven to prove him wrong...rather, I was always fearful of proving him right...

To begin living life without excuses...to **get your head our of your "but"** you must dig down to the root of it all. In other words, you must excavate the essence of your "but". Begin to think of all the reasons (justifiable or not) that have been permitted (by you) to choke out the hope of your future. Imagine those reasons/excuses/your "but" showing up in your past – perhaps as far back as your youth – with no other intention than to plant in your mind the premise that *you just can't do **it**.*

Close your eyes...visualize your "but" standing in an open field with a shovel beckoning your destiny to a shallow grave and enticing it to jump in. Look deeper. From where did that "but" come? When was that seed of doubt planted in your heart, spirit, or mind? By whom? Find the origin of it and cut off its life source so that you can begin to walk out God's purpose for your life. Until the root is obliterated your "but" will continue to linger making it easy to conjure excuses for your stagnation.

    Inability to move forward is the biggest hindrance to future development. Until the causation of that inactivity is identified you will remain incarcerated by your "but"; you become an "enemy of the state" of your life. I think one of the most difficult realities of being a prisoner is the knowledge that freedom is just beyond the prison walls but is in no way within reach or grasp of the one incarcerated. Seeing the daylight peer through a small window at the very top of a jail cell is the constant reminder that there's something out there far greater than what's inside.

Unfortunately, until you break free from the restraints of your "but" you are likened to that prisoner. You know your purpose and destiny are out there but you're stuck behind a wall of "but" that is preventing you from experiencing the freedom that comes with standing up to your "but".

Without freedom, you are stuck…not in the here and now…rather, you are stuck in your past – that is, as far back as the inception of your "but" – you are bound there. Moving forward just isn't an option.

When your destination seems further from view today than it did two weeks ago you have to take time to evaluate your "but". You must ask yourself, "Why is it that I seem to be treading water? What is it that's weighing me down so that I'm running fast but seem to be marking time? I'm standing still, going nowhere, stagnant!" I can see how this becomes frustrating and even, at times, very discouraging.

Never having taken the time to dig up your "but" and its source only holds you further back as life, around you, continues to move forward. The good news is, now that you have been challenged to glare into the mirror of your life and your past, identifying and dealing with your "but" gives you the authority to enter into the progression of your fate.

Don't become angry with everyone around you if you refuse to deal with your "but". Don't fall into the slump of regret and despair because you have been abducted by and held hostage to your "but". Rather, identify your "but" and determine that today is the last day you will allow your thoughts and plans for tomorrow to be ordered, directed, or controlled by your "but". I implore you, **_get your head out of your but_**!

You are obligated to your right now and your future. The obligation you bear is to no longer be bound by the negatives that have been hovering over your life; take courage, take on the strength of God which is made perfect in your weakness (II Corinthians 12:9); break the chains of the bondage of your "but"; walk freely, confidently, boldly into the you that has been buried under the first and every "but" that was bestowed upon you, even against your will.

You must remember that stinking thinking…begets stinking thinking…begets stinking thinking…begets unfruitfulness, regret, and eventually a dream that becomes buried…it dies, either in you or with you. Whichever is the case, your "but" will have smothered every possibility of you *becoming* rather than simply *existing*…chew on that for a moment.

Can you see how your "but" brings about a limitation on your desire and even your purpose? How often have you found yourself contemplating your "but" in greater detail than your plan to overcome the odds pitted against you? The only person that can defy your "but"...the only person that can ***get your head out of your but*** is YOU.

Don't be deceived, though. Understand that your "but" can be singular or plural! This process of finding the essence of your "but" could be one, that must be repeated multiple times. What am I saying? Don't be blind to the "but" that's been lingering and laying low as you go after the blatantly obvious one. Scroll through the rolodex of your mind; take time to really dig deep so that every "but" is exposed, eradicated, and expelled from your life.

Make the choice to occupy your thoughts with the promise and hope of your prosperous future. Be intentional to guard yourself and your mind against every thought or purpose that stands in opposition to where you are going. The Bible encourages, in Philippians 4:8, to think on the things which are of a good report...with the authority given by God, I encourage you to do the same.

Did you know your "but" only cares that your mind is so consumed with *it* that you can't focus on anything else? Have you ever had a puppy that wanted you to expend all of your energy on it? Remember how he would chase in front of you (sometimes tripping you) when you raised from the couch just to ensure he wasn't left out of your next step? What about when you would try to take a nap and he'd snuggle up close to you? Now, remember how you cuddled him and nurtured him...even though he sometimes got in the way?

Your "but" does the exact same thing(s)...the only difference is your "but" is nowhere near as cute as your puppy – so why do you cuddle it as such? It's nowhere near as cute as your puppy – so why do you lend so much attention to it? It's nowhere near as cute as your puppy – so why has it exhausted you to the point that you have no energy for what really matters (your purpose)? Your "but" not only snuggles next to you when you sleep, it infiltrates your dreams and holds them captive until you break its wicked bonds. Your "but" is dark, ugly, dismal, and each time you raise up to do something great, it chases out in front of you (***always*** tripping you) to ensure it's not left out of your next step.

The essence of your "but" is the very core of what persuades you away from anything greater. The power of your "but" is that it consumes your thoughts; it highjacks your vision; it arrests your purpose. This is why the urgency exists to **get your head out of your but**.

Why is your "but" so powerful? Perhaps it's been ingrained in you from your youth. Perhaps you've "failed" so many times that the only option is to surrender to your "but". Perhaps your family dynamic points to the reality of your "but" more than it illuminates your ability to obtain God's purpose for your life. Perhaps you've exercised your "but" so much that its muscle is greater than your unattended destiny.

Identify what fuels your "but" and cut off the source immediately! Contradict the false reality presented by your "but" (I will cover, in greater detail, effective contradictions in Chapter 5 *Kiss Your But Goodbye*). The possibilities of where you can go become choked out by the impossibilities that loom in the shadow of your "but".

The truth is that your "but" has been a dark force in your life far too long. Dark, why? Because it blinds you to your future. Imagine all that you were afraid to accomplish because "but" stepped in the way. Think about every dream that was shattered because "but" showed up. Now, think harder about from where that "but" stemmed.

My But

I'll share an example of how family dynamics can presuppose "but" in and on your life. I graduated from high school in 1995 with no real plan for my future. I wanted to go to college, yet, didn't see how that would happen financially. During that summer after graduation, I made the decision to join the US Army.

January the following year I became enlisted, a soldier, uncertain about life, now coming into a plan for my future. I determined that I would make this a career, retire young (age 38), and still have time to pursue much more. I was excited and nervous all at the same time – oddly my nervousness was not so much because I had enlisted into the Army, rather, more so because I finally had a plan.

I went to Basic Training and graduated. Then I went to Advanced Individual Training (AIT) and graduated. After that graduation, I met up with my family members at the Virginia state line as we were on our way to my brother's wedding. Awaiting at the state line was: my mother and father, twin sister, aunt, and a few cousins. I remember this day vividly because it, perhaps unintentionally, changed the trajectory of my newly planned life.

I must go before the following details by saying that when I was a child the side of my father that I experienced was the polar opposite of the man he later became. Several years before my father's death the Lord saved him, changed his character and his life and he became an extremely kind, caring, and compassionate man.

…We met at the Virginia state line and began to hug and love on one another. When my father hugged me, the words he spoke in my ear shattered my very core, "I'm proud of you... ***but***, you'll never be as good as I was." *OUCH*! It pierced, it stung, it hurt...it became the standard up to which I lived. You see, all of my military leaders saw greatness in me and they tried to pull it out. They saw me as a leader among my peers and wanted to give me the opportunity to fulfill that role. *But*...those words kept ringing in my head "you'll never be as good as I was".

When that was spoken over me I outwardly said, "I'll show you"; but inwardly the dagger cut too deep; my motivation to succeed was being choked out. I held up the universal sign for choking and seemingly no one ran to my rescue. Perhaps that's because my words betrayed the pain I felt inside and my actions betrayed my words. Let me explain: with my lips, I said, I'll be the best me that I can be, but my heart was devastated and refused to press beyond that hurt. Therefore, my actions lined up with my heart rather than my verbal boast of becoming great.

While stationed in Dexheim, Germany my Platoon Sergeant, First Sergeant, and Sergeant Major all pushed me and encouraged me to go before the promotion board. They all believed I would make a great Non-Commissioned Officer (NCO). I was afraid…I didn't want to fail…only because they pushed me, I went. Not only did I go before the promotion board, I scored the highest of all candidates that day.

After passing the promotion board with flying colors, I became "promotable". There were still some things that needed to be done before I could get my "stripes" and I was determined NOT to do those things. Understand, my "but" was so loud in my ear that I refused to muster the courage to take those critical steps toward my future.

I was then stationed in Ft. Carson, Colorado where my Platoon Sergeant, First Sergeant, and Sergeant Major (a totally different Chain of Command from that in Dexheim, Germany) insisted that I attend the Primary Leadership Development Course (PLDC). I went…kicking and screaming the whole way! When I arrived there (Ft. Lewis, Washington) the instructors saw in me what all of my other leaders saw and they immediately made me the Student First Sergeant. I was petrified! Instead of my confidence rising it was on a steady decline.

Even though all of those people around me were pushing me to greater, I was held captive to my "but" and was on a continual progression to sabotage my future. When I left PLDC and returned to my duty station (Ft. Carson, Colorado) my fear level was significantly amped. I made up my mind, "I won't take the final steps to get this promotion…I'll just get out of the Army". That was it…the final hurrah.

I began out processing and I signed my papers for ETS (Expiration – Term of Service) from the Army…as an E-4 (P) – that means promot***able***. I never got my stripes and I never retired. After only 5 of the required 20 years, I left my dream behind all because of my "but". Those words my father spoke had power over me. I was never driven to prove him wrong…rather, I was always fearful of proving him right…I had become discouraged, dominated, and defined by my "but".

The Challenge

Your challenge for the remainder of this chapter is to connect with your dream, embrace your purpose, define your destiny…and then, I want you to identify your "but"…stand face-to-face with what's high jacked where you're going and bound you to where you are, next dig deep to expose the essence of your "but". Be intentional to take time with this exercise; be honest about every "but". Remember, this is all about excavation so dig deep…I want you to get to the root of every "but" that has leeched onto your dreams and seemingly drained your future.

Your Dream(s)	Your "but"	The Essence of Your "but"
To retire from the Army	I won't be successful	My father told me I would never be as good as he was

Chapter Two

The Dis-Qualifier

...the more credence you give to that destiny killing "but", the less likely you are to break free from low confidence...

In sports, athletes may have to qualify for certain events by meeting set standards which correspond to their weight, gender and/or age. It's obvious, yet worth stating, that to qualify athletes must first show up. If they fail to show up, they have already dis-qualified themselves from the event. It's as if the no-show, qualified athlete is saying, "Don't consider me for this one."

When an employer posts an announcement for a job they specify the required qualifications for the position. Job seekers who happen upon the announcement see how, or if, they measure up to the qualifications posted. If a person who meets the qualifications refuses to apply because they fear someone with more experience or better education will beat them out, that person immediately dis-qualifies themselves before they ever have an opportunity to be considered by the hiring manager.

Because of the cancelling properties of "but", it is able to make its bearer question their own worth and cause a person who is most definitely qualified to dis-qualify themselves. You see, "but" says that although you may feel that you are just as qualified as others, maybe even more so, your "but" makes that feeling null and void. It's almost like your "but" is a big pink eraser. It's waiting patiently for you to muster the courage to finally acknowledge your purpose, plan, or destiny, and then before you can visibly see it written, your "but" jumps in and removes all traces of that acknowledgement. Please, TODAY, determine to **get** *your head out of your "but"*, everything that lies ahead of and for you depends on *that* determination.

So often I've found myself restlessly sitting on the sidelines of my own life; pushed aside while other "characters" took center stage and played the starring role in my life. It's not as if I was unaware of my assigned role in the script. I can't say I didn't know my place. Rather, I feared what taking my place would yield. Greater expectation? More responsibility? Greater exposure? Success??? What!!!???

I determined I'd just step back and let others shine instead. After all, they were much prettier, smarter, had better ideas, and were more liked than was I. Remember what I stated in Chapter 1, "stinking thinking…begets stinking thinking…begets stinking thinking…begets unfruitfulness, regret, and eventually a dream that becomes buried"…well, I'll be the first to admit, I was stinking up the place!

Your "but" becomes a confidant to and a place of solace for your confidence – or lack thereof. The more credence you give to that destiny killing "but", the less likely you are to break free from low confidence. As I became intentional to excavate my "but(s)" and to identify the essence of each one, it became much more clear the many times I've dis-qualified myself because my confidence confided in my "but" and made it difficult for me to step out…my feet felt like concrete cinder blocks, my mouth felt like it was full of cotton, and my heart felt like it was racing in the Indy 500. As qualified and equipped as I knew I was, my "but" encouraged me to dis-qualify myself time and time again.

I confess that even as I am writing this book I am fighting through several degrees of self dis-qualification. I have to keep reminding myself that what God has placed inside of *me* to say must be said. Every so often, I have to shoo away that "but" which says, "There's someone out there who is far more qualified than you to write this book." Trust me, I know…the struggle, albeit unsolicited, is very real. Nevertheless, the desire to press through it must be determined and unending.

Have you ever tried to move forward and been met by a roadblock? Did you press and persevere only to find that roadblock was you? So many times, I found all that was standing in my way was me and my self-sustaining "but". So many opportunities in ministry, academics, career, and life in general…

I consider all that I didn't reach for because of my dis-qualifying "but". Can you relate? Can you acknowledge that there have been things in your life that you didn't consider yourself for, even when everyone around was cheering for you to proceed? Don't kick yourself because of lost opportunities…instead, thank God for the second, third, or fourth chance, to self-reflect and redeem the time you feel you've lost…or even yet, the time you feel you've wasted.

My But

When I was a little girl I always knew I wanted to be a pediatrician when I grew up. You know, people bend over and ask, "What do you want to be when you grow up?" My enthusiastic response, without fail or hesitation, "A PEDIATRICIAN!" My oldest sister is 9 years my senior. When she was away at college my mother sent my twin sister and me to visit with her during the aftermath of Hurricane Hugo. While there, we went to classes with her and when asked by one of her professors, "Young ladies, what do you want to be when you grow up?" As always, as if on cue, I responded with a big smile, "A pediatrician!"

It felt good knowing what I wanted to be…"BUT"…upon further consideration, I didn't really feel smart enough and what if a child came to me that I couldn't help? The biggest enemy of my perceived purpose at that time was my self-contrived "BUT". You see, as children we have an innocence and a faith that is insurmountable. Can you identify that somewhere along the way you lost the faith to believe that you could *be* or *do* what God placed in our heart to *be* or *do*?

Not only did I magnify my "but" (not feeling smart enough), I believed it so much that I allowed it to manifest in my life; I dis-qualified myself before the race even began. I went from being an honor roll student to barely doing well enough to progress to the next grade. Often, I struggled to succeed in academics. Not because I couldn't, rather, because I was afraid of the subsequent demands of that success. This vicious cycle followed me throughout my formative years and beyond. Think about that. Formative is a word that describes something that made you who you are…"something that makes you who you are". For me that was….a self dis-qualifier.

The formative years are those years that played a major role in the person you are today. As you reflect on your "but" was it something that was birthed, nurtured, and developed in your formative years? Has it been with you so long that it only seems *natural* to keep it around? Have you magnified its significance such that it has seeped into other areas of your life? What, where, who has your "but" caused you to dis-qualify yourself against?

The Challenge

Revisit your "but(s)" from the previous exercise and any that you may have remembered during this chapter. Think about what your "but" may have dis-qualified you from. Document it here. Remember, the time you feel you've lost coddling your "but" can certainly be redeemed as you surrender it to God. As you add "but(s)" to this exercise, be sure to go back to the previous chapter to document the dream attached and the essence of your "but".

Your "but"	The Dis-Qualification
I won't be successful	• Promotions • Successful career in the Army • Retirement at a young age
I don't measure up	• Academic success in my formative years • Pursuit of my dream to be a pediatrician • Growth in ministry

Chapter Three
The Distortion of Your But

…step from behind the defensive wall and see your "but" as the weakling it really is…

You have to acknowledge that your "but" is in the way of, and blocking the course of where you are going. The wall of "but" is in front of you and you have a decision to make. No one can pull you over that wall because if they do, then your "but" will be on your back. Understand, there is a huge difference between putting your "but" behind you and having your "but" on your back. I want you to leave it behind you because, even on your back, it drains your energy and has an expectation that you have made reservation for it in your mental capacity.

When I served in the US Army, I had the fortune (or misfortune) of going on countless road marches. The road march was sure to consist of numerous inclines and extremely long distances and were primarily done as a part of a field exercise. As a soldier, my preparation was to pack my duffle bag and rucksack. The difference between the two was that my duffle bag could be tossed with one hand, always seemed limp in comparison and was left "in the rear" while my rucksack, with its predefined packing list, felt like a ton of bricks and was carried on my back.

I always needed help with putting my rucksack on, and without hesitation, someone gladly assisted. The initial mounting of the rucksack on my back always gave me a bit of a jolt. Once we started moving, though, it didn't seem so bad. I would begin to adjust to the heavy load that refused to release me, shifting the weight as needed to continue the march – sometimes even moving the heavy sack to my front as opposed to my back.

After walking about 1/6 of the way into the road march, though, my legs would start to wobble and what was once easy to carry, soon became a troublesome weight. Not only was it heavy physically, this weight began to take a toll on my mental capacity as well. I'd begin wishing I could have left it behind (in the rear) with my duffle bag.

Liken the weight of that ruck sack to the heaviness accompanied by your "but". That load, at times, can seem unbearable to the point of wanting to quit. However, why quit when the more profitable option is to drop the load? Why quit when, after releasing your "but" your legs will strengthen and your stance will become firmer? Why quit when shedding the weight of your "but" also frees you from its dizzying affects?

If you quit, you still have to deal with that weight because you are quitting with it still attached. Consequently, even pressing through the quit is difficult because the haze of your "but" is right there with you. Please, walk away from it and leave your "but" behind you.

Anatomically you are made such that your "butt" is at your rear or behind you. Please explain to me why it is, then, that metaphorically, you insist on putting your "but" in front of you – much like I did with my ruck sack. It gets in the way; interferes with your footing, and even impedes your view.

This leads us to the distortion of your 'but'. This pesky twerp sees you coming and sticks his foot out to trip you…and you fall for it every time. Understand, your "but" puts a haze over your vision so that you cannot see what God has purposed for you. I often tell people, even if you can't see you have to still have vision. How, though, can you have clear vision with the haze of "but"? Your "but" distorts your view making it very difficult to see where you are going.

Think about the times you've distorted the reality of your "but". You give it more credence than it's worth; you magnify it far bigger than the magnification of your purpose. You breathe life into your "but" rather than curse the root from whence it came. I agree, "but" can be scary and because of that fear it appears much larger than it really is.

Consequently, we have all fallen into the snare of cowering in the place of familiarity and the comfortable place; even if that place really isn't so comfortable. I challenge you today to step from behind the defensive wall and see your "but" as the weakling it really is.

Maybe someone assisted you in donning your "but". Perhaps they encouraged you that it fit just right. Or, could it be your "but" is magnified because it was introduced to you when you were only a child? From that perspective, everything appears larger than life!

As you matured, your perception of your "but" was never re-evaluated because you accepted way back then that it was much larger than you and even larger than what you could be. Step out today and stare your "but" in the face. I guarantee you will find yourself LOOKING DOWN because your "but" is nowhere near the size or velocity you've depicted it to be in your mind!

Your "but" is so clever and multifaceted that even as you are making it larger than it really is, your "but" is distorting the reality of who you are and how you see yourself. You see, when "but" takes its place in your life it settles in comfortably and quickly begins to distort your view of life, and more detrimentally, your view of yourself. How so? We've heard it said that "your perception is your reality" and we can all agree that this bears much truth. If you perceive your "but" as this strong giant, that means you perceive yourself as a weaker, smaller being than it.

Consider the spies Moses sent out to assess the land of Canaan. He instructed them to see how many people were in the land; assess the strength level of the people there; determine if the land is good or bad; what are the residential structures like there; check out everything and bring back a report (read Numbers 13-14).

Moses sent out twelve spies that day. The returned report of the majority was an unfavorable one. They said the people are strong and the city is fortified and…the people are **huge**! However, two of the twelve (Caleb and Joshua) were confident they could overtake the land. See, God had already promised the land to them *but* the majority of the spies were fearful of what they saw; they lacked the confidence to confront the distortion of their "but". In fact, they said, "we were **in our own sight** as grasshoppers, and so we were in their sight". Take note of that important detail. Because the spies viewed themselves as grasshoppers, their perception was that the people of Canaan must view them the same way.

This report ravished the camp of the children of Israel and they began to embrace eternal defeat in the wilderness. Their "but" had distorted their vision such that they were willing to forfeit the very thing God told them they could have. The end result, as expressed in Numbers 13:37, was that those ten spies who brought the contrary report were in fact defeated by their "but" …they died in the wilderness. Because they couldn't put their "but" behind them, where it belongs, they couldn't see beyond it…it distorted their vision and obstructed their ability to gain possession of their intended destiny.

It will prove beneficial for you to read the referenced chapters in Numbers; yet, I will note that Caleb and Joshua did not suffer the same fate as the ones who were in captivity to their "but".

My But

This chapter is about the distortion of your "but"; in Chapter 1 we excavated our "but(s)" and in Chapter 2 we identified those things from which we have dis-qualified ourselves because of our "but(s)". Keep in mind you can have several "buts" that have contributed to your way of life and who you have become today.

Understand that even as I write this book, I am diligently recalling the "but(s)" that God has delivered me from. I want to share with you a "but" that distorted my view for many years and in more ways than one. Please permit me to be real, relevant, and raw with you without you casting a judgmental glare.

I remember saying to one of my best friends, "If marriage didn't call for sex I would be comfortable living with a female for the rest of my life". The look on her face told of her discomfort as she reluctantly, yet narrowly, agreed. I had to immediately chase down where this thought, this logic had been hatched. It didn't take too long for me to surmise, it all stemmed from my "but".

This "but" was dear to my heart, I held it close to my bosom because if I shared the details of it no one would fully understand and perhaps they'd put me in a predefined box rather than really hear me out. This "but" I nurtured and cared for because no one else seemed to care or even able to. This "but" I wrestled with because even I didn't understand the awkward grip it held on my life.

I can't say I ever asked, "God, why me"? Naw, that never crossed my tongue or my thoughts. I did, however, ask how to overcome.

You see, when I was just a little girl (8-10 years old) I was molested by an older male. A part of his deviance was to not only violate me, he also made me do things that were intimate and sexual in nature to other girls as he watched. Please understand, I've never been confused by nor struggled with my sexuality. I've never had a fondness or attraction for women BUT there was this thing that had been planted in me long ago that the enemy attempted to use to distort, or confuse, my identity.

You see, this thing that was done, this seed that was planted made me question my true identity and my future propensity for years. Consequently, in addition to "but", I struggled with "what if"!

I remember always dreaming of falling in love with a wonderful man, getting married, and having children. I came really close to that dream becoming a reality too. When I moved to Colorado in 1999, I met a gentleman who loved me unconditionally. He was the only man (at the writing of this book) who ever actually *dated* me. I found myself falling in love with him...BUT...what if that seed which was planted when I was a little girl manifests itself? What if I begin to struggle with my sexual identity? I pushed him away...FAR away.

This "but" was attempting to distort the core of who God made me... my very identity was at stake. Since then I've had other "relationships" but none have led to the fulfillment of my dream. I can say today that struggle is over, I only pray God sends true love my way again. I pray the distortion of my "but" those many years ago has not rendered me a continued future of doing life alone. However, I am completely yielded to God's plan for my life.

Another distortion which was a consequent of this "but" was how I perceived the gentleman who violated me.

Because he had overpowered me and robbed my vulnerability, I saw him as a big and muscular guy. I thought he was huge! Every time I saw him, my view of myself in comparison was that I was very small, weak, defenseless – this distortion lasted well into my adulthood. Why? Because I never took the time to re-evaluate my "but"; I never stepped from behind that wall to see it for what it really was; in many ways, I was held hostage to my "but".

In 2012, I began to pray about what that "but" really meant to me and the depths to which it impacted me, my life, my future. When my father died in November of that same year I saw the gentleman for the first time in years. I looked at him with a sense of pity and I thought, "Gee, is he sick? He looks so small…hmm". I asked my sister if he looked sick to her or different, I said, "Wasn't he really built and muscular when we were kids?" She said, "No, he's always been scrawny". Wow, in that very moment, I could see clearly…I felt a victorious triumph over my "but".

The Challenge

Consider the "but(s)" you excavated in the previous chapters. Your challenge for the remainder of this chapter is to acknowledge the distortion you have suffered as a result of your "but(s)". Feel free to add to your list if more "buts" come up as you read and complete the challenges.

Take your time with this exercise, cry if you need to, and end it all with a prayer of surrender to God. Rid yourself and your destiny of the toxins associated with your "but(s)" and assume clear vision once the distortion is exposed. As you add "but(s)" be sure to go back to previous chapters to identify the dream attached and the essence and the dis-qualification of your "but".

Your "but"	The Distortion of Your "but"
I won't be successful	• I was so afraid of proving the source of my "but" right that I cowered when the opportunities presented to prove him wrong
I don't measure up	• I viewed myself as insignificant and unqualified for many advancement opportunities
I was molested	• I feared embracing true love • My molester appeared much larger and stronger than he actually was

Chapter Four
Clear Your Headspace

...sometimes stinking thinking just feels like the easy and least complicated frame of mind to possess...

Your headspace, your state of mind, your mindset deserves to be free of degradation and recurring doubts that are fueled by any "but". You owe it to your fast approaching destiny to flush the waste and garbage from your headspace. Reserve that space for thoughts of the promising future God has for you. Allow everything you've come through, every inhibiting "but" you've been freed from, to catapult you to a life of great fulfillment and purpose.

Sometimes stinking thinking just feels like the easy and least complicated frame of mind to possess. It really doesn't require much…just a lazy, unproductive, mindless…thought. Yes, there will be times that you have to be intentional to refocus and redirect your thought process. You will experience moments that you must bulldoze the space in your head that has become overdeveloped by every "but" and the residential squatters it brought along.

When guests overstay their welcome, you begin to feel a sense of overcrowding that you didn't feel prior. It seems everything they say or do, now, irritates your nerves to the point that you just want them gone…immediately! Upon their arrival you warmly welcomed them and said, "Please, make yourself at home". You cooked, sat up to watch movies, laughed, and enjoyed the much-needed company. However, you look up and they've been there three days beyond the agreed upon stay. Hmm…it's about time for your once "welcomed" guests to move along…the welcome has long since expired.

What do you do? You've asked them to leave and they laugh you away. Now what? Your requests for their departure becomes demands as you stand your ground in every effort to clear your residential space of individuals who have assumed occupancy in a place to which they do not hold the title or deed.

When you open the door for your "but" to hang out in your mind, over time you will begin to feel the same sense of overcrowding. It is essential to where you are going that you set an expiration date to your "but". I would even advise that you set a date that has already passed or that is soon to come so as to intensify the urgency of evicting unwelcomed, or no longer welcomed, inhabitants. You have to acknowledge that the bondage of you to your "but" remains in perpetuity until you determine enough is enough.

Clearing your headspace requires a determined effort to abandon self-defeating and self-sabotaging thoughts and instead adopt the thoughts suggested in Philippians 4:8. Contemplate things that are true, just, pure, lovely, and of a good report. For many of us, this type of thinking doesn't come naturally…to strain out every "but" occupying space in your head, it is imperative that this way of thinking be ushered, by you, to the forefront of your mind.

Fog is, in essence, a cloud that touches the ground and can make it impossible for you to see what is ahead of you. Brain fog is a very real companion of your "but". Brain fog can, and will, preclude your ability to visualize your purpose-filled future. Brain fog can, and will, slow your travel as you gingerly feel your way from one mile to the next. Brain fog can, and will, separate you from your present reality. By intentionally clearing your headspace, ridding yourself of brain fog, and evicting "but", you make the choice to be present in your life. After all, it is about time you take center-stage and assume the starring role in what God has scripted to be your life. You cannot be the star if, in fact, you are not present. Please, today, **get your head out of your "but".**

It is imperative that you assume the role of a school principal and expel every "but" that has no other objective than to violate your peace and to disrupt your focus. Imagine, now, the clarity of mind you will have after eliminating toxic pollutants emitted by your "but" over the years. Just pause, take a deep breath, as you release that breath close your eyes and visualize a headspace that is free of "but"...visualize and *hear* the chains of bondage to every "but" being shattered and crashing to the floor. You may get emotional – that's quite alright. Lay your head back, take as long as you need, and embrace this moment...

Chapter Five

Kiss Your But Goodbye – The Final Battle

...the last time was the last time you surrendered your purpose to the burglarizing menace of your "but"...

Here it is, the chapter you've been waiting for. This is the last ounce of attention you are permitted to give to your "but"...the final kiss because this kiss says GOODBYE. In this chapter I want to share with you contradictions to every "but" that has leeched on and been your uninvited "ride or die". I can only introduce these contradictions to you; it is incumbent upon you to activate them in your life.

This is about to be the ultimate role reversal. All these years your "but" has contradicted your confidence, motivation, and every dream. Well, today and every day going forward, you are going to be the bearer of halting contradictions. No longer will you travel the course outlined by your naysaying "but". The last time was *the last time* you surrendered your purpose to the burglarizing menace of your "but".

You will be confidently equipped to stare your "but" in the face and denounce its power in and over your life. The weapon of I CAN and I WILL is sure to give you unimaginable strength to quickly deflate the air-filled and delusionally larger-than-life "but" that has, in uninvited form, taken control of and overshadowed your life.

Consider the reality that your "but" is an enemy to your purpose and destiny. The most effective way to combat an enemy of this magnitude is to be properly equipped for the battle that has been on going long before you realized you were drafted to the front line. This is significant because you've been taking blows and are only now coming into the understanding of why you keep getting hit. Well, now you know, and GI Joe said, ***"knowing is half the battle".***

Now that you have dug up your "but(s)" and realize the adverse effect they have had, are having, and will continue to have on your life and where you are going, it is time to gear-up and engage the enemy. You see him, he's in your sights…your greatest challenge, though, is that he sees you too and he now knows that you see him. It's okay, you've got this…time to armor up!

As you prepare for battle you must be well aware of the importance of protective armor. God gives descriptive detail of the armor you should don in preparation for this battle (read Ephesians 6:14-17). Understand, each piece of armor covers vital areas of significance as it pertains to your purpose and your destiny. Proper use of this armor is critical to your success in the fight to contradict your "but(s)". In brief, the armor consists of: the belt, the breastplate, the shoes, the shield, the helmet, and the sword. Although these all work simultaneously to ward off the detrimental effects of your "but", let's explore the significance each one bears and how to effectively use each one when contradicting your "but". This marks the moment you begin to pucker up and to kiss your "but" goodbye.

The Belt (of truth)

The intended purpose of the belt is to hold all the other pieces of the armor in place. The belt is positioned at your center, or your core. Here, is the essence of who you are and your very uniqueness. The core of you houses your strength and your resounding truths. Protection here is critical because nothing should be permitted to shake you at your core.

The Belt (of truth) serves to hold together your commitment to truth and to oppose the lies you coddle. The Belt (of truth) contradicts your "but" by setting you free from those lies. Your "but" would have you believe you can't obtain the promise from God of your future, purpose, and destiny. The truth says, however, that "all the promises of God in Him are Yes, and in Him Amen" (II Corinthians 1:20). Your "but" exclaims that you can't do it. However, the truth proclaims that "with men this is impossible, but with God all things are possible" (Matthew 19:26).

With the Belt (of truth) you are now equipped to identify the lies associated with your "but(s)" and speak relevant truths to discredit their worth and weight in your pursuit. No longer will the lies of your "but" stunt your growth, arrest your dream, or impede your stride. Going forward, tighten the Belt (of truth) around your core and debunk the lies of your "but" by making a new commitment to your resounding truths.

The Breastplate (of righteousness)

Protected behind the Breastplate (of righteousness) are the vital organs. Vital organs are those ones that are absolutely necessary for life – the heart, the lungs, the liver, and the kidneys. Damage to any one or combination of these has extreme consequences and can lead to death. Think about that metaphorically in relation to your "but" and your future. Each of these organs can be correlated to some aspect of your soon coming destiny. You must be mindful of the damaging affects an accurate aim can have and how your "but" can bring about death to your destiny.

The arrows of your "but" are accurately aimed and piercing. When it takes aim the intended target will likely be hit. The Breastplate (of righteousness) provides cover and protection from deadly blows to those critical organs. Your heart circulates blood through the body. Your lungs oxygenate the blood, pulls in fresh air, and gets rid of stale air. Your liver filters the blood that comes from your digestive tract before it is passed to the rest of the body. Your kidneys filter blood to produce urine and prevent a buildup of waste in the body.

    Take inventory and make note that each of these vital organs deal, in one way or another, with your blood. Blood is that fluid in the body which provides necessary nutrients and oxygen to the cells and carries away unnecessary waste from those same cells. Detriment to any of the vital organs will, in fact, affect the flow, circulation, or intended properties of the blood. Again, let's look at that metaphorically in relation to your "but". Your purpose-filled destiny is what fuels your drive and your motivation. However, every "but" cuts the circulation, suffocates the air, clogs the filter, and deposits deadly waste products into the cells of every action required for you to move into your destiny.

The Breastplate (of righteousness) is that defense which counteracts the deadly blows of your "but(s)" to the vital organs of your destiny. It breathes new life (fresh air) to the hope of your future "the Spirit of God has made me, and the breath of the Almighty gives me life" – (Job 33:4). It purifies that hope by eliminating waste that has been deposited or has not been properly filtered.

Understand, without the Breastplate (of righteousness) you leave your destiny wide open for certain devastation from fatal attacks. Conversely, as you don the Breastplate (of righteousness), you take on the righteousness purchased by Christ for you. This is the purification which washes away the debris and junk left behind from every "but".

The Shoes (of the gospel)

The right pair of shoes make walking feel peaceful and a pleasure. However, even with the right pair of shoes, obstacles can be challenging at best. The Shoes (of the gospel) is that part of the armor that helps your footing, even on rugged terrain. Your "but(s)" set stumbling blocks in the way of your path with the hopes of causing you to trip/fall, give up, and turn back. However, wearing the Shoes (of the gospel) gives you a spring in your step that allows you agility with every encountered obstacle – "…He will make my feet like deer's feet, and He will make me walk on my high hills" (Habakkuk 3:19).

The Shield (of faith)

As daggers are thrown, it is imperative to have some defense in place to stand between your destiny and those daggers. The Shield (of faith) serves as that defense. You see, your "but" knows the hope you once had to pursue your purpose and is launching an all out attack in an attempt to make you abandon that hope. Well, with the Shield (of faith) you are able to intercept those blows and, thereby, strengthen your hope – "…I have prayed for you, that your faith should not fail…" (Luke 22:32). Being equipped with the Shield (of faith) gives you the strength to believe again.

The Helmet (of salvation)

Your head can be considered the most vital part of the body because it houses your brain (thought and mind). It's been said that the greatest internal battle a person ensues is in their mind. You see, your thoughts are always with you and unless you are able to pull the reins and gain control of those inhibiting thoughts of "but", they will quickly send you spiraling.

The Helmet (of salvation) ensures coverage of the head. Proper use of this part of the armor equips you to be persuaded in your mind by God and not distracted by the thoughts once conjured in response to your "but". Knowledge of where you are going will not be easily swayed by the deceptive woos of your "but". "…How long will you falter between two opinions? If the Lord is God, follow Him; but if Baal, follow him" (I Kings 18:21).

The Helmet (of salvation) is also vital to the protection of your ears. It is imperative that you guard your gates (the ears being one of them). The deception of your "but" can ring loudly in your ear. All the more reason to properly don the Helmet (of salvation). The closer you get to obtaining your destiny the louder your "but" will scream in your ear. Don't give in to this deterring tactic which ultimately leads nowhere. Be encouraged, "Let no one deceive you with empty words…" (Ephesians 5:6).

The Sword (of the spirit)

Your only weapon, the Sword (of the spirit) is what you will use to gain victory over your "but(s)". As you review the armor outlined above, you will recognize that this part is the only part that puts you in an offensive position; all other parts of the armor serve to defend you against the attacks launched by your "but". For this reason, all contradictions to your "but" are scriptures – that is your Sword (of the spirit) – "For the word of God is living and powerful, and sharper than any two-edged sword, piercing even to the division of soul and spirit, and of joints and marrow, and is a discerner of the thoughts and intents of the heart" (Hebrews 4:12).

Don your armor, put on the confidence of God and in one final act of faith, blow a kiss as your "but" becomes a fleeting memory in your past.

Chapter Six
A Time of Reflection

...take whatever amount of time is necessary to dig up and properly discard of every "but"...

Your "but" can now be considered a thing of the past; it should be behind you where it belongs. Remember, there is an identifiable root to every "but". Some may take longer than others to expose. Even if you did not target every "but" as you worked through the exercises in this book, set aside time to do so until you are free from the clutches of each one. You owe it to yourself and your future to take whatever amount of time is necessary to dig up and properly discard of every "but" forevermore.

Keep in mind, some of your "but(s)" might be painful to face and, some, even painful to let go. Remain prayerful through this process as you attain for the purpose-filled destiny that belongs to you. Be encouraged and know, you are not in this alone.

From the Author

Thank you for making the investment to purchase your copy of this book. My genuine prayer for you today is that you are able to connect with its message for the sole purpose of seeing beyond where you've been, breaking free from what has held you captive there, and chasing into all that God has purposed and planned for your life, your future, your ultimate destiny. My final words of encouragement to you are simply:

Get Your Head Out of Your But!

Humbly,

Merica A. Green, M.A.

Additional Worksheets

Your Dream(s)	Your "but"	The Essence of Your "but"	The Dis-Qualification	The Distortion of Your "but"

Your Dream(s)	Your "but"	The Essence of Your "but"	The Dis-Qualification	The Distortion of Your "but"

Your Dream(s)	Your "but"	The Essence of Your "but"	The Dis-Qualification	The Distortion of Your "but"

www.ingramcontent.com/pod-product-compliance
Lightning Source LLC
Chambersburg PA
CBHW031205090426
42736CB00009B/798